The Ultimate Business Card:

Promoting Your Business Through Authorship

Norene Broyton

© 2014 by Norene Broyton

ISBN-13:978-1495414862

ISBN-10:1495414868

All Rights Reserved.

All Rights Reserved.   No part of this publication may be reproduced in any form or by any means, including scanning, photocopying, or otherwise without prior written permission of the copyright holder.

First Printing, 2014

Printed in the United States of America

Disclaimer/Legal Notice
The information presented represents the view of the author as of the day of publication. Due to the rate at which conditions change, the author reserves the right to alter and update the information based on new conditions.

This book is for informational purposes only. While every attempt was made to accurately state the information provided here, neither the author nor her affiliates or publisher assume any responsibility for errors, inaccuracies or omissions. Any slights to people or organizations are unintentional.

The Ultimate Business Card:

Promoting Your Business Through Authorship

The Ultimate Business Card

Dedication

This book is dedicated to small business owners everywhere. Your expertise and dedication to your customers is what makes your community strong!

Norene's Website: http://norenebroyton.com

The Ultimate Business Card

Table of Contents

Is A Book Business Card Right For Me and My Business? 9
Types of Book Business Cards 13
   How-To Books 13
   List Books 14
   FAQ/SAQ Books 15
How to Create a Book Business Card 17
   The Parts of the Book 18
      The Book Title 18
      Cover Design 18
      The Content 20
   Editing and Formatting 21
      Formatting For a Kindle Book 22
      Formatting For a CreateSpace Book.......................26
   Publishing 28
      Publishing a Kindle Book........................... 28
      Publishing on the CreateSpace Platform 30
Promoting Your Book Business Card 37
Done For You Service 39
Conclusion 41
About the Author 43

The Ultimate Business Card

Is A Book Business Card Right For Me and My Business?

Thank you for picking up my book, ***The Ultimate Business Card: Promoting Your Business Through Authorship***. This book was written for those who have never written a book before but would like to have a book to showcase their expertise and/or business. I have tried to cover everything that you need to successfully write a book that would benefit your business. It is difficult to foresee every issue that may arise when writing a book or detail every possible piece or nuance in one book. Therefore, throughout this book, I have referenced whenever necessary that more detailed information can be found on my site http://norenebroyton.com. If you have questions about anything in this book, you can also contact me through that website. Updates will be posted there as well.

If you are a consultant, a coach, a speaker or a small business owner, you should consider authoring a book. Imagine for a moment that you are looking to buy or sell your home. You meet Bob. He is friendly and enthusiastic. He appears to be knowledgeable. After chatting for a bit, he hands you his business card and you leave. His business card has his name and phone number. Perhaps it also has his hours of business and perhaps a catchy slogan. The next day you meet Sara. She also is friendly and enthusiastic and appears to be knowledgeable. Upon leaving she hands you a book that she has authored titled, *"Seven Easy and Affordable Fixes That Will Increase The Value of Your House by 20%."* Or *"Five Pitfalls to Avoid When Buying Your First Home."* With all else being equal, which realtor would you most likely hire? Which "business card" would you more likely look at again after receiving it?

Being an author in your field immediately gives you credibility and authority. Others will see you as the expert that you are and having a book will help you stand out from your competition. It also gives you a way to provide instant value to your potential customers, establishing trust. You can distribute your books in person or online, thus increasing your reach. You can give away your book for free, or you can sell your book for additional revenue. Finally, people pass along books to their friends, extending its reach even further.

Today when self-publishing is available to anyone, I firmly believe that everyone should author a book. Everyone has at least one area of expertise to share that would benefit others. Below are just a few professions/businesses that would benefit from a Book Business Card:

- ❖ Bakers/Bakeries
- ❖ Chefs/Restaurants

- Chiropractors
- Consultants
- CPAs
- Dentists
- Dieticians
- DJs
- Dog Trainers
- Electricians
- Event Planners
- Financial Planners
- General Contractors
- Hair Stylists
- Home Improvement Specialists
- House Painters
- Landscapers
- Massage Therapists
- Mechanics
- Occupational Therapists
- Orthodontists
- Personal Trainers/Gyms
- Physical Therapists
- Plumbers
- Pool Builders
- Reading Specialists
- Realtors
- Roofers
- Speakers
- Tax Preparers
- Tutors
- Vets
- Website Designers
- Wedding Planners

While I firmly believe that anyone can write and publish their own Book Business Card, I understand that many people would prefer to spend their time running and growing their business. For this reason, I have created a Done For You service. More information can be found at the end of this book or on my website http://norenebroyton.com. If you choose this affordable option, you could have a book authored by you, in your hands within a matter of a few weeks.

Types of Book Business Cards

So now that you see that a business card in the form of a book could benefit you and your business, the next step is to decide what type of book makes most sense. If you are still thinking that there is no way you can write a book, remember that it doesn't have to be long. You can (and should) choose just one very specific topic that you feel would bring great value to your customers. That is the key. What piece of knowledge or know-how do you possess that they would value the most? Brainstorm topics by thinking of questions you are asked most frequently. From that list you can create:

How-To Books

A *How-To* book can provide exceptional value to a potential client. Perhaps you are a landscaper. You could write a *How-To Book* on the best or fastest way to trim hedges. A dog trainer could write a book about house training tips. A pastry chef could write about how to make the perfect piecrust. As an expert in your field, there are hundreds of valuable tricks and tips that you could share with an audience that is dying to know. You do not need to give away all of your knowledge, just one very specific how-to that your potential clients would appreciate.

One of the biggest benefits of writing a *How-To Book*, in addition to being extremely valuable, is that in many cases the bulk of the book can be pictures, not words. If you do not fancy yourself a writer, you can perform the task that you want to teach and have someone photograph each step as you do it. You place those pictures sequentially in a book, with detailed instructions under each photograph, and you have a book that is even more valuable than if you had just written about the topic.

You do not need to worry about giving away so much valuable information that the person will no longer have a need to hire you. What you are sharing is just one sliver of knowledge, to showcase your expertise and instill trust. This is something that a typical business card cannot do.

List Books

A *List Book* is also a very easy book to create and depending on the topic, can be extremely valuable to your audience. A *List Book* is simply that: a book that lists information. A DJ could create a book that lists favorite songs for different occasions. Perhaps it would contain a list of favorite songs for wedding receptions, a list of popular songs for high school dances, etc.

A friend of mine was a high school English teacher and became a consultant to teachers after 30 years in the classroom. She created a book of writing prompts. A teacher could pick up this book and have hundreds of writing prompts to choose from to give to her students to write each day. This Book Business Card has landed her many speaking engagements and consulting jobs.

A wedding planner could create a *List Book* in the form of a checklist. Each page could be dedicated to a different part of the planning that the bride and groom needed to complete.

As you can see, a *List Book* could provide immense value to a potential customer, while being quite easy to write and publish.

FAQ/SAQ Books

A *Frequently Asked Questions* (FAQ) or *Should Ask Questions* (SAQ) book can be an excellent resource for anyone trying to determine if a service is right for them. An orthodontist could write a *FAQ/SAQ book* for parents listing answers to questions that parents ask most about braces, i.e., the cost, the duration, or how the need is determined. A mechanic could write a *SAQ Book* on the types of questions a car owner should ask before getting repair work done.

A quick way to write this type of book is the Interview Technique. This involves creating a list of questions about the topic and then having someone ask you these questions. As you answer, they can either write down your answers or you can speak them into a recording device. Once finished, you would just need to transcribe the tape or polish up their notes.

Bear in mind that these are just three examples of books that can be created as a Book Business Card. There are no rules to this – it is your book. You can choose an example from above, or create a book based on a different format that works best for your area of expertise.

How to Create a Book Business Card

The first step in creating your book business card is to decide what type of book you want to write. If you haven't yet read the previous section, take time to do so and decide if you want to create a *How-To Book*, a *List Book*, a *FAQ/SAQ Book* or something different that makes sense for your service/business.

Next you need to decide if you would like your book to be a physical book, a digital book or both. A physical book makes sense if you will be meeting with potential clients, going to conferences where you can distribute them, or if you would like to sell them passively from a bookstore or an online store such as Amazon. A digital book makes sense if you have a website where your potential clients can download it, or again if you would like to make passive sales from places such as Amazon's Kindle store or Barnes and Nobel's Nook store. You may want to create your book in both formats.

Once that has been decided, you need to consider the different parts of the book creation process. These include writing, formatting and publication. Throughout this book I am going to explain how to create your digital book business card for the Amazon Kindle and, for the paperback version, through their CreateSpace program. I chose these because they are straightforward to use. However, there are many different places to publish a digital book and a physical book. If you choose a different alternative, just follow their guidelines. Much of what is written here will still be applicable.

The Parts of the Book

You can put together your Book Business Card in any order that you wish. You will need a strong book title, an engaging cover design, and the content.

The Book Title
The title of your book will say a lot about you, so take some time to consider different titles. Do you want something that is quirky or engaging? Do you want something that simply tells the reader what the book is about? Regardless, the cover should clearly indicate the content. If you choose a clever title, you may want a content-oriented subtitle that speaks directly to the topic. Perhaps a plumber would create a book titled, *Stopped Up Again? Five Tips to Unclog Your Drain.* A good title should be concise, clearly convey the main topic and attract readers. Brainstorm a number of titles and ask others for their opinion.

Cover Design
Some people choose to save the book cover design until the book has been written. Others create their cover first. It doesn't matter. Depending on the topic of your book,

you may want to have a picture of yourself or something that represents your area of expertise. A realtor, for instance, may have a picture of a house with a sold sign on the cover. A landscaper may have a picture of landscaping that he personally created. Whatever you decide, there are some important aspects to keep in mind.

1. Your cover is the first impression that people have of the book and *you*. Take your time with this piece. You may want to create several different covers and ask others their opinion.

2. If you choose to have a picture on the cover, you need to own the copyright. If you take the picture yourself, this is not a problem. There are websites where you can download pictures for free to use as long as you give attribution to the photographer. Personally, I would stay away from these sites and choose instead a site where you can buy the rights to the photo. Some of my favorite sites include: http://fotolia.com, http://istockphoto.com, and http://shutterstock.com. Even with these sites, it is important to read the terms and conditions before using the photograph on your cover or within the content of the book.

Creating Your Own Cover With Photo Editing Software

If you are familiar with photo editing software such as http://photoshop.com or http://www.gimp.org, you will be able to create your own cover. The benefit to doing this yourself is that you do not have to wait on someone else to create it and you the design will be exactly as you want.

The downside is that it can take a good chunk of time to create.

Creating Your Own Book Cover Within Create Space

Amazon has made it fairly simple to create a professional looking book cover through their cover creator within CreateSpace. The cover that is created can be used for both your Kindle book and your paperback book. The steps on how to do this can be found in the section on creating your paperback book (page 32). The downside to this option is that the templates are not very flexible.

Outsourcing The Book Cover Creation

If you are not familiar with photo editing software but you want more flexibility than what CreateSpace's cover creator will produce, you may want to consider hiring someone to create the cover. Experts can be found at freelance sites such as http://www.odesk.com, http://elance.com or http://99designs.com. Prices may range from $25 to several hundred dollars for a good book cover.

The Content

Since you are an expert in your field, writing the content for your book should be the easiest part. Creating the document can be done with software such as Microsoft Word or Open Office. Regardless of the type of book you are writing, it is helpful to start with an outline. If you are writing a *How-To Book*, make a list of all of the steps involved. Try to be as detailed as possible. Remember – you are the expert and may do several of the steps without even realizing. It can be helpful to have a non-expert in your field read what you have written to ensure that it is complete.

For a *List Book*, the outline would include different categories. Going back to the DJ example, the author may have the categories, Romantic Songs, Slow Dance Songs, Line Dance Songs, etc. By creating an outline, the writing becomes easier and it helps ensure that nothing is left out.

In addition to the content of your book, you will also need a title page and a copyright page. Depending on the style of the book and personal preference, you might also have a dedication or acknowledgements page, a table of contents, a preface, and an afterword. As an expert, you may have local articles about you and your work or magazine articles or blog posts you have contributed to. Include references to these in your book as well.

Finally, make sure that you provide the reader information about you, your services and how to get in contact with you. This may include your Facebook page and/or website address, and your physical address and phone number. Those who are interested in your business and services need to be informed about how to find out more.

Editing and Formatting

Once you have written, revised and perfected your book, it is important to have someone else edit it. A second or third pair of eyes will ensure that it is the best book possible. Remember, this book is an extension of you and your expertise. You don't want grammatical errors, misspellings, missing content or poorly constructed sentences. It is well worth it to pay someone to go over your manuscript before moving on to formatting. If you do not know someone personally, you can hire an editor from http://www.odesk.com or http://elance.com or other freelance sites online.

It doesn't matter if you choose to create your digital book first, or your paperback book first. Many times I create the Kindle book first because in it you can have links to websites and other parts of the book. I find it easier to take those out when transferring to the Create Space layout, than it is to put them in if I were to go from the CreateSpace layout to the Kindle layout.

Often times, however, I do create my book cover in CreateSpace prior to publishing my Kindle book. The cover maker in CreateSpace, although not yielding very creative covers, can make cover creation easy and by creating them there, you can have both your Kindle cover and your CreateSpace cover match. If you are outsourcing the cover creation, then it really does not matter which book you choose to create first. Again, you do not need to have both a digital book and a physical book, but I wanted to cover both formats in case you choose to have both.

Formatting For a Kindle Book

Formatting a Kindle book has caused many an author to pull out their hair. To me, the beauty of Kindle is that less is better. Special formatting, page numbers, headers and footers are not included in a Kindle book. Special fonts are also not needed. "Serif" type fonts such as Times New Roman are perfect, and due to the size of a Kindle, you don't want to use a font larger than 12 for the main text, or size 18 for headings or subheadings.

Kindle Template

You can obtain a Kindle template from my website http://norenebroyton.com. You do not need to use this template, but it does make things a bit easier. It has a Block paragraph style, which means that the first line of each paragraph is not indented. It also has the margins pre-set.

TOC in a Kindle Book

If you need a Table of Contents (TOC) in your book business card, it is preferable to have one that links to each chapter via a hot-link. This makes it easier to navigate your eBook and provides a better experience for the reader.

There are two ways to create a functioning TOC in your Kindle book. The first is the manual way through bookmarks. To insert bookmarks, you would place the cursor at the chapter or sub-chapter heading and click on *Insert>Bookmark*. Then name your bookmark something like C1, C1a, C2, C2a, etc. Then you go to the beginning of your document and type out the list of chapter titles. For each one, highlight and right click. Select *Hyperlink*, select *Place in this Document*, and choose the bookmark that corresponds with the chapter.

The automatic way is to go to *References>Table of Contents>Insert Table of Contents*. Since the default is to show the page numbers, you want to uncheck the *Show Page Numbers* box because there are no page numbers in eBooks. This process will automatically create a hot-linked TOC based on the headings and subheadings throughout the book.

If you use the Kinstant Formatter tool (see page 25), it will create the TOC for you based on your heading styles. There is an option during the conversion process to Add/Replace TOC. If you check that box it will import a hyperlinked TOC for you.

Other Kindle Tips

There are other formatting tips that are often overlooked for those new to publishing an eBook. I have found that the eBook looks better when every chapter is started on a new page. You can add links throughout your document by highlighting what you want linked and then right clicking and selecting Hyperlink from the box that pops up. Choose *Existing File* or *Web Page* in the menu on the left and in the *Address* section type in the full link, including the http:// part. This is what makes it clickable.

You can include images throughout your eBook. You do this by going to *Insert>Picture* and then browsing to find the appropriate picture. **Remember that you must have permission to use all of the pictures that are in your book**. You should use the "In Line With Text" setting for the images. You can choose the "center" option afterwards if you would like the image to be centered on the page. Kindle prefers images that are 300 dpi, and that are BMP, JPG or PNG.

Acceptable Document Formats

Amazon makes it possible to upload a Microsoft Word .doc file directly to the Kindle platform. You can also upload an HTML, which can be created by choosing *Save As > Web Page, Filtered* when saving in Microsoft Word. If you are using a Mac, you choose *Save As>Web Page*. If you are using Open Office, you just *Save As* to HTML.

Most people upload a PRC format, which can be created using a conversion tool called Mobipocket Creator, which is owned by Amazon. Another option is Calibre (http://calibre-ebook.com/), which is a free tool. It is beyond the scope of this book to delve into how to use Calibre, but a free guide can be found at http://www.makeuseof.com/pages/download-open-book-managing-your-ebooks-with-calibre.

A paid alternative to format a document into the mobi format is Kinstant Formatter. I have used this tool and find that it makes formatting my books correctly a breeze. The benefit of using either Calibre or Kinstant is that you can see right away if you have any formatting errors and then make the necessary changes before uploading the book to the Kindle platform.

To recap, a Word Document, HTML, PRC, and Mobi are all acceptable formats to upload to Kindle.

Previewing Your Kindle Book

There is a preview option within the Kindle publishing platform, but I prefer to preview my book before uploading. You can do this by download the free Kindle Previewer software that is available on Amazon for both the PC and the Mac.

If there is anything that does not look right, go back and change it. Once all looks good, you are ready to publish your Kindle book (see page 28).

Formatting For a CreateSpace Book

Using Amazon's CreateSpace service allows the average person to create a paperback book. Amazon's specifications for formatting can be found their site. Once published, you can buy as many books as you would like at cost, to distribute to your potential customers. The book will also be listed on the Amazon site for anyone who is interested in the topic to buy. When they do, you will receive a royalty of about 40% of the book price.

Formatting for a CreateSpace book is easier than for a Kindle book. You can choose the size of the book you would like to create. The most common is a 6"x9" book. Templates for the various sizes can be found on my blog at http://norenebroyton.com. If you choose to use these templates, the margins and gutter have already been set, making it easier to have a properly formatted book. It is just a template, however, and you can change whatever you would like. I would suggest you make a copy of the template to use so that the original template remains untouched.

Pay attention to the disclaimer in the template. It is just a placeholder to remind you that one is needed. It would be wise to consult an attorney to create a disclaimer that is appropriate for your book and its contents.

If I have already created a Kindle book, I start by copying the contents from that Word document and pasting it into the CreateSpace template. If not, I begin to write my book directly on the copied template.

From there, I take out any linked information and replace it with the actual text. For instance, if I had a link going to google.com, I would replace that link with the actually site address, such as http://google.com. If I had a link going to a different part of the book, I would reference that part of the book. For instance if I had a link going to Chapter 1, I would take that out and state instead, see Chapter 1.

In a physical book, the TOC is not hyperlinked. You will need to replace the Kindle TOC with a TOC that has page numbers listed. This is as simple as removing the TOC and reinserting it. When this is done, since page numbers, as part of a TOC is the default, you will have a TOC with page numbers listed.

If you choose the 6" x 9" size book, I would suggest using the font size 12. I prefer to keep the font to New Times Roman, but you can change it if you like. Go through each page and make sure that it looks right. Start each chapter on the right hand page, starting a few inches from the top.

Just like in the Kindle version, you can have pictures in your paperback version. For CreateSpace, color photos add to the cost to produce the book. It will be up to you to determine whether the cost is prohibitive. Often if I feel that color photos are necessary, I will create the book with them in and then upload it to CreateSpace to see what the cost will be. I can then make an informed decision as to whether to keep the color photos in, or reformat them as grayscale to bring down the cost. Instructions on how to reformat pictures from color to grayscale can be found in this book's section on the Book's Interior (see page 32).

When your document looks good, go to *Save As* and choose PDF from the drop down menu. This is the file extension that you need for CreateSpace.

Publishing

It is a different process to publish a book to Amazon Kindle and to Amazon CreateSpace. Below I will detail both. The process for each has not changed much overtime, however, Amazon's instructions are detailed, so you should not have any problems following their guidance if the process changes. They also have good support that you can email if you have questions regarding publishing.

Publishing a Kindle Book
In order to publish your eBook on the Kindle platform, you need to create an account at Amazon KDP (http://kdp.amazon.com). You can sign in with your

regular Amazon account, or if you don't have one, you can create one there. You will be prompted to update your information, which is necessary to begin earning money from your eBook.

Once that is done, you can click on the *Add a New Title* button. A new window will open where you will add all of your book details and upload your files. You will also have the option to participate in KDP Select if you would like to. KDP Select allows you to put your book into the Kindle Owner's lending library for 90 days. During this period of time you can also select 5 days to make your book free. If you choose KDP Select it will renew automatically after the 90 days unless you go into your Bookshelf and un-enroll it from the program. If you choose to place it in KDP Select program, you cannot have your eBook advertised for sale anywhere else on the Internet, including your own website, during those 90 days. There is no restriction, however, about publishing the physical book to various locations during that time period.

Pricing Your Kindle Book

You can price your Kindle book at whatever price you would like. If you price it under $2.99 or over $9.99 you will receive 35% of the sale price. If you price it between $2.99 and $9.99 you will receive 70% of the sales price. If you are using your book as an opportunity to gain future clients, you may want to price it low to attract as many people as possible. You can choose to have your book available only to those in the United States, or throughout the world.

Once you have saved your book details and clicked on *Publish*, you will get a pop-up notice that informs you that it may take up to 24 hours for an English language book to appear in the Kindle store and 2 to 3 days for a non-English book to appear. You are then prompted to go to your Bookshelf. At that point you are done. You will receive an email from Amazon once your Kindle book is live.

Publishing on the CreateSpace Platform

Getting Started

To publish on the CreateSpace platform you first need to have an account. This is a different account from your Kindle account. Go to http://www.createspace.com. Click on the *Sign Up* button to sign up. You will need to provide an email address, a password, your name, your country and what you plan on publishing (a paperback book, a CD or a DVD). Once you have accepted their terms they will send you an email message to verify the account.

Once you have verified the email, you can come back to CreateSpace to publish your book. You have the choice of doing it yourself or talking to a consultant. The set up process is relatively easy. Amazon walks you through each step.

The first step is to set up your account information and your payment preferences. Again, if you sell any of your books through Amazon, you will receive a royalty.

After that is complete, you will see a menu on the left-hand side of the page. From that menu choose *Add New Title*. You will be walked through what is needed. You will need to fill in the title of your book under *Tell Us the Name of Your Project*. You will choose what type of project you are creating. Choose paperback. You will then be asked if you want to be guided or not. Choose *guided* so that you don't miss any steps.

At this point a new screen will appear where you will put your name as the author and the description of your book, a subtitle if there is one and a volume number. You can leave both of these blank if there is none. Click on *Save and Continue*.

The next screen is to choose an ISBN. You can choose an Amazon ISBN, which is free. If you goal is simply to sell your book through Amazon and to hand out books that you have purchased yourself to your potential clients, this option is fine. If you choose the Custom ISBN or the Custom Universal ISBN you can list yourself as the publisher imprint, but you cannot print your book elsewhere and it doesn't make all of the distribution channels available that you would have if you used the free Amazon ISBN or provided your own ISBN. For these reasons, I would suggest either the free ISBN or the last option, which is providing your own ISBN.

Once you have the ISBN, you should go back to your paperback book document and include it in the manuscript. You will need to then save it again as a PDF document.

The Book's Interior

At this point, you will be taken to a page where you describe how you would like the pages of your book to look. This is where you choose whether or not you want the pages to be white or cream and whether the book will be entirely black and white or if there will be color (text or images). Color adds significantly to the price of the book, but depending on your content, it might be worth the additional cost.

If you had color images in your Kindle book but do not want to pay the additional cost for color in your CreateSpace book, you will need to go back to the CreateSpace manuscript and change the color images to grayscale. You do this by clicking on the image, choose *Format Picture>Recolor>Grayscale*.

At this point you can choose to *Upload Your Book File*. By clicking on this option, you will be directed to find your PDF document on your computer. Once you have done so, it will upload your file and after a few minutes it will tell you if there were any errors. At this point you can preview how the book looks and see the errors it has referenced.

If everything looks right, you can continue to the next step. If there are issues that you would like to resolve, you can modify your manuscript, save it as a PDF again and upload it again. You can do this as many times as you would like until you are satisfied with the outcome. Once you are satisfied, you click *Save and Continue* and it will take you to the Book Cover page where you can design or upload your book's cover.

Creating the Book Cover

Amazon makes it possible to create a book cover right inside of the CreateSpace platform. You can also upload your own cover or hire their design team if you would like. The easiest option is to hire their design team (https://www.createspace.com/Services/CustomCover.jsp), however this service currently starts at $399. You can hire someone on a freelance site such as http://odesk.com or http://elance.com to create a cover for you, which may cost less. If you are good at design, you could create your own. You need to keep in mind the dimensions that are required. These are listed within CreateSpace's help pages and are based on the number of pages, the book size and type of paper that you choose. You will need to make sure that the dimensions include the book's spine and back cover.

My preference is to use the CreateSpace book cover wizard. Within this wizard you can choose from among 30 different templates. Once chosen, you will be directed to add a picture (must be at least 300 dpi) and you can choose from among several different fonts. You can also add a picture of yourself to the back cover (must be 300 dpi) and write a bio. The major downside to using their wizard is that the options are limited. I have, however, created several covers this way and have been pleased with the outcome. You can also use the cover that you created with the CreateSpace cover wizard as your Kindle book cover. If you would like to do this, please visit my website at http://norenebroyton.com to learn how.

Submitting Your Book For Review

Once your book cover is created, you will be taken to a "setup" page where you will verify the details of your book. After this has been completed you will submit your book for review. At this point, the title of your book gets locked in and you will not be allowed to change your book size. If this becomes an issue, you can start the process all over, creating a "new" book, with a different ISBN.

While under review you will not be able to make any changes. During this time a CreateSpace employee verifies that all of the files are printable. They do not check for any editing issues, so they will not catch typos or missing content. Proof reading is left up to you.

Within about 48 hours you will receive an email indicating whether or not your files have been accepted. If it was not accepted, the email will tell you why and you can go back and fix any errors and resubmit. If it has been accepted, you will be taken to a page where you can download a digital proof of the book and/or order a print copy. I always do both. The digital proof you can view immediately. The printed copy, which will arrive within a week to ten days for those living within the United States, is a second check to make sure that everything looks good.

Once you accept the proof, your book is listed within the Amazon store (if you have chosen that distribution channel), usually within 24 hours. If you have a Kindle version as well, the books will be linked. This means that if someone posts a review of your Kindle version, that review will show up on the paperback's sales page as well.

It also means that if someone lands on either book's sales page, they will see that they can order either your kindle version or the paperback version.

Setting Up Distribution Channels

After you submit your book for review, you can set up your distribution channels. By default, your book will be available through Amazon.com, Amazon's European sites and the CreateSpace eStore. On the distribution channel's page, you can opt out of any of these locations if you so choose.

You can also pay $25 for expanded distribution, which gives you the option to sell your book to bookstores and other online retailers, libraries and academic institutions.

Pricing Your Paperback Book

Amazon immediately sets up the cost to produce and distribute your book. If you choose to buy copies of your book at the wholesale price, this is the price you would pay, plus tax and shipping. If you price your book higher than this, you will receive from 40% to 80% of the price. When you type in the amount you would like to sell your book for on the Pricing Page, it will tell you how much per book you will make.

The Ultimate Business Card

Promoting Your Book Business Card

Once you have your Book Business Card created, you need to decide how you will promote it. Perhaps you created just the paperback version and your plan is to hand them out to potential customers that come into your place of business. If this is the case, you just need to make sure you have enough books on hand.

Perhaps you want potential customers or clients to find your book through you personally as well as online. If this is the case, you may want to advertise your book. You can create a press release and submit it online alerting the news media of your book. Oftentimes local media will pick up the story bringing in more publicity and business. There are dozens of online press release sites. Some of my favorite sites include: PR Web, Web Wire, PRlog and Press Method.

You can also promote your book along with any advertising you already do. You can place a QR code on a flyer or newsletter that, when scanned, will lead directly to your book on the Amazon or Kindle store. If your business is on social media, you can alert current and future customers by linking to your book in a Facebook update, a picture on Pinterest, or through your Twitter or LinkedIn account.

Done For You Service

As I stated at the beginning of this book, I feel that any business or service can benefit from having a book business card. It will set the business apart from competitors and showcase the owner's expertise and range of services. Creating a book is time-consuming, however, and it may be hard to justify the learning curve to create just one book.

For this reason, I have created a Done For You service, whereby I work with you to create your book. After gathering the content, I design and write the book, from cover to cover, with your name as the author. Your time commitment is minimal, and you can have a professionally written book created affordably and ready to distribute within a matter of weeks. If you are interested in pursing this option, please visit my website, http://norenebroyton.com for more information.

As a special thank you for purchasing this book, a 50% discount for this Done For You Book Business Card service will be applied, if ordered before March 14, 2014. Just mention that you bought this book when you contact me.

The Ultimate Business Card

Conclusion

Creating the Ultimate Business Card can quickly set you apart as the go-to expert in your field. Whether you create it on your own, using the information in this book and on my website, or use the Done For You option, your Book Business Card will enhance your business for years to come.

The Ultimate Business Card

About the Author

Norene Broyton has written and published dozens of best selling books in a variety of niches under several pen names. She has now branched out to help speakers, consultants and small businesses create their Ultimate Business Card. For a free consultation on how this service could help you share your expertise and land more clients, please contact Norene through her website, http://norenebroyton.com.

Printed in Great Britain
by Amazon